John Fletcher Williams

The Groves, and Lappan: Monaghan County, Ireland

An account of a pilgrimage thither, in search of the genealogy of the

Williams family

John Fletcher Williams

The Groves, and Lappan: Monaghan County, Ireland
An account of a pilgrimage thither, in search of the genealogy of the Williams family

ISBN/EAN: 9783337290306

Printed in Europe, USA, Canada, Australia, Japan

Cover: Foto ©ninafisch / pixelio.de

More available books at **www.hansebooks.com**

THE GROVES, AND LAPPAN;

[MONAGHAN COUNTY, IRELAND.]

AN ACCOUNT OF A PILGRIMAGE THITHER,

IN SEARCH OF THE

GENEALOGY OF THE WILLIAMS FAMILY.

By JOHN FLETCHER WILLIAMS,

Secretary of the Minnesota Historical Society ; Corresponding Member of other Historical and Genealogical Societies.

PRIVATELY PRINTED FOR THE FAMILY.
SAINT PAUL.
1889.

" *Je viens de faire un ouvrage.*

   Comment ? un livre ?

   Non ! pas un livre. Je ne suis pas si bête."

ONE HUNDRED AND FIFTY COPIES.

PREFACE.

*To my Kinsmen and Kinswomen of the Williams
Family:*

It has doubtless been known to you that for
some years, I have been much interested in the
history of our family, and have gathered from
every possible source, all the facts regarding it,
which I have been able to discover. In that pur-
suit, I have spent no little time and labor, and
considerable means, the latter at least $250—no
remarkable sum, of course, but it shows that genealogical researches are expensive, and that I
have spared no means of doing the work thoroughly.

A journey to Europe in 1888, gave me a long-
coveted opportunity of visiting Wales and Ireland, and pursuing my genealogical investigations at the very cradle of the family. I there
gathered so much important and interesting information regarding our family, that I deem it my
duty to place it in the hands of those members of
the same, who are interested in our history. I
have therefore had printed a few copies of my col-
lections, simply for the use and gratification of the
family, and to preserve the facts from loss. An-

other object of this publication was the awakening of more attention to the subject of family history, a science which is in late years assuming great importance in sociology, and furnishing valuable facts in the study of heredity.

It is not, strictly, a genealogy, and I do not call it such, for it is far from being complete, as I have been able to bring it down only to the seventh generation. But it has material which some one, in the future, with the requisite leisure and means, can weave into a complete history of the family, such as will do the latter a credit. These are simply preliminary notes, which I print in this shape, to save the labor of answering the numerous letters I have received, asking about the results of my researches in the old country. I offer them merely for what they are worth.

Truly Yours,

J. Fletcher Williams.

St. Paul, Aug. 1889.

NOTE.—The small figures attached to the names of members of the family, indicate the generation to which said family belongs.

THE WILLIAMS FAMILY.

THE only definite and (presumably) reliable account of the earliest ancestors of the Williams Family, which was in possession of the family for many years, was that recorded by the late Samuel Williams, of Cincinnati, Ohio, who, in the beginning of his manuscript memoirs, which he wrote about 1850, stated, as a legend, (received from his father, William Williams,) that the earliest known ancestor of our family was "supposed to be one John Williams, (though his given name was not positively known), a hatter by occupation, of Glamorganshire, Wales, who had been one of those persons who advanced funds to aid Oliver Cromwell in the conquest of Ireland, in 1649, and who, after the subjugation of that island, went to Ireland, where he received from the Protector, in return for the above advance, and possibly for military services, a grant of lands, probably a portion of the confiscated lands of the rebels, and settled on the same. It was supposed that this land, or a portion of it, was the same estate that was subsequently known as 'The Groves,' in Monaghan County, where the family resided for nearly two centuries."

It is remarkable how this family legend, or tradition, handed down orally from father to son, through several generations, was found, afterwards, to agree with the real facts of history, re-

garding the origin of our family, and is now sub-
stantiated by actual records, (since found). Samuel Williams was not in a position, when he wrote
in 1850, to push his investigations to a point where
he could get any definite and tangible clue to the
genealogy of our family, for which, however, he
left such valuable material on record in his memoirs. He had no access to any documents, in the
archives of Great Britain, and had no means to
make a pilgrimage to the ancestral home, a de-
sideratum accomplished by one of his sons, 38
years subsequently.

Who Was Our Ancestor, John Williams?

The untiring investigations of historians and
scholars in later years have thrown valuable light
on many events concerning which but little was
known when Samuel Williams wrote his memoirs in 1850, and has made it possible to prove
definitely and clearly what was before merely
surmise.

Some 25 years ago Mr. John P. Prendergast, an
attorney of Dublin, began an investigation of
some old manuscript documents in the Tower of
that city, with a view to ascertain facts regarding the Cromwellian Invasion of Ireland. He
secured a large amount of material whose existence was hitherto unsuspected, and soon after
published a historical work on the era above
mentioned, entitled:

"The Cromwellian Settlement of Ireland."

Among other documents which Mr. P. discovered and prints in his interesting work is the original "List of Adventurers" as they are there termed, of which our ancestor John Williams, was one. The history of this movement may be briefly given as follows:

The "act of parliament, 17 Charles I, chap. 33, A. D. 1642," and subsequent acts, had authorized a scheme for suppressing the Irish rebellion by forfeiting two and a half million acres of Irish lands which were to be offered as security to those who should advance moneys towards raising and paying a private army for subduing the Irish rebels. The subscribers, or "adventurers" as they were called, were to have estates and manors of 1,000 acres each given to them in Ireland of various prices in the several counties, ranging from £200 to £600, and lands proportionably for less sums. The rates by the acre were to be 4 shilling in Ulster, etc. On the "List of Adventurers for lands in Ireland," etc., published in Prendergast's work, we find a subscription as follows:

919   John Williams, ffeltmaker £50

The term "ffeltmaker," of course, is synonomous with "hatter," which we know was the hereditary occupation of the family for seven generations.

After the suppression of the rebellion in Ireland, the confiscated lands of the rebels were distributed to the discharged soldiers who had taken part in the conquest, and to the subscribers to the fund. It must have been under this apportionment that "John Williams, ffeltmaker" was granted his estate in Ireland. As it was located in Ulster, he would have received for his £50 subscription about 250 acres. Whether this tract was the same or not, subsequently known in the history of the family as the homesteads called "The Groves" and "Lappan," which are now shown on the official maps by those names, we have not now the facts to determine, but it is almost certain that it was the same, since "The Groves" was certainly the seat of the Williams family very soon after the close of the rebellion, and remained permanently in their line for over 150 years.

The Williams Family In Wales—Its Origin, and Meaning of the Name.

John Williams, "The Adventurer," was a descendant of one of the oldest families in the principality of Wales, and which had long resided near Neath, Glamorganshire. It is useless and unnecessary, therefore, to search for the etymology of our name in the languages of any other race but the Cymbrian. The name "Williams" is entirely Welsh (so far as our stirps is concerned), and the family are indubitably of ancient Briton or Cambrian stock, for generations back. The name, in the Cymbrian tongue, is derived (says Dr. Alex. Jones, an eminent Welsh scholar), from the verb *"gwylio"*—to watch. The noun of this verb is *Gwilym* (pronounced William) and would therefore mean—a watcher, a sentinel, a guard, a warder, a patrol, etc. The name, (as applied to a person), evidently arose from a military occupation, as it was one common in Wales at that period, and belonged to a large class, which can be readily understood, by any one who reads the history of Wales, its frequent and almost constant wars, its predatory raids from rival chieftains and princes, and foreign foes, together with frequent domestic broils. To give timely notice of these invasions, and collect the trusty men-of-arms who should repel the foe, the princes and military leaders were accustomed to have, on their towers, and other points, trusty sentinels. There were also stationed on mountain cliffs and summits, near the sea-coast, and at the head of defiles, to spy the advancing invaders, and signal the danger. Each *Gwilym* was to light a beacon fire on the first sign of alarm. This was answered from another mountain peak, and then another caught up the warning flame, until, from every hill top over a whole county, blazed the signals of danger, calling the men of arms to buckle on their swords and saddle their steeds, and rally at the accustomed rendezvous.

The post of "gwilym" was thus one of danger and responsibility and no one was trusted to perform it except one of undoubted bravery, unswerving patriotism, and proven fidelity. Perhaps this may have had much to do in impressing on the family for generations, during which this post of honor, (for it was generally hereditary) remained in the clan, that warm and unaffected patriotism, unswerving fidelity to duty, and faithfulness to every trust, which has always been a characteristic of the family.

Further Notes on the Name Williams.

Though the Welsh, or original British race, are a very ancient people, and probably came from Asia many centuries ago, the exact time when the word, or name, "Williams," became a fixture among them, is now only conjecture. In the Domesday survey of England, (1086) the word William, as a surname, occurs 6S times, but generally in such a form as this, "William, filius Ricardi." or "William, son of Richard." Some centuries later this would become, "William Richardson." The names *Willelmus* and *Willielmus* also occur in the Domesday. As William the Conqueror was then popular and powerful, it is natural that many sons of influential families should be named for him.

The name "Williams" (as we write it now), is not, however, of great antiquity, for it has been used as a surname only about four centuries. Its earliest mention in the records and archives of Great Britain, was about the middle of the 15th century. I think that in every case, in that period, it referred to a native of Wales. Still, I find in the "Carew Manuscripts" (relating to affairs in

Ireland), date 1571, the expression "Williams Sept," indicating that there was a clan or tribe of the name there then, but it seems certain that they must have been incomers, and not natives of Ireland, as the name is not found in ancient Irish archives.   A careful examination of Burke's genealogical works, the "Peerage" and the "Landed Gentry" of Great Britain, seems to prove that but few of the oldest and most distinguished families of the surname "Williams" can trace farther back (under that name) than 1600.   One lineage, in Burke, speaks of a Williams born in 1473 (reign of Henry VII), but it is not certain that he used our surname, as Burke, in another pedigree, mentions a Roger Williams in the time of Henry VIII (1543) who, he says, "was the first of the family who adopted a surname of any kind."   In the lineage of another family, he speaks of a"William Williams, who was the first of the family who assumed the name of Williams."   In 12 Edward IV., (1472) a Sir David Williams is recorded as living in 1490.   Thus it can be seen that the surname "Williams," as a permanent family name, did not come into use much over 400 years ago. This was about the date that printing was invented.   "Williams" is given as one of the characters in Shakespeare, in King Henry V, act 4, scene 1, (1413-1422).

The orthography of the name, at first, does not appear to have been well fixed.   In an old pedigree in the Harleian MSS., (date about 1620,) the

name is spelled *Gwilliams*. Burke, in his genealogical works, frequently spells it *Gwillym*. Geo.
T. Clark, a Welsh genealogist, in his great work
on Glamorganshire pedigrees, always spells the
name *Gwilim*. The family of Roger Williams,
the founder of Rhode Island, (A. D. 1550–1650),
used to spell their name, *Wyllyams*, and subsequently *Willyams*, Roger himself so writing it
in his earlier life. Many families in England
still spell the name thus.

The name became a very common one in Wales.
In the city of Neath, Glamorganshire, I believe
that quite one-half the inhabitants bore the name
"Williams." They have been prolific authors, too.
In the great catalogue of the British Museum, I
found 116 pages of a folio volume, devoted to the
list of books written by authors of our name.
Lower, author of a learned work on Patronoma-
tology, says that 21 different surnames are derived
from the name "William."

The Name "Williams" in European Countries.

In Florence, Italy, I saw the name "Guglielmi"
engraved on the door plate of a pew in a gorge-
ously decorated Jewish synagogue. This name
means *Williams*, in the Italian tongue. I also
find persons of the name Guglielmi, Guglielmo,
and Guglielmini, Italians by birth, mentioned in
the *"Biographie Generale."* This name is from the
mediæval Latin word "Gulielmus," or the name
William, though I feel sure that the former is but

the latinized form of the German Guilhelm, as it
is certain that the name Gulielmus was not known
to the old Romans.

In one of the MSS. of the Public Record office
in London, I found a document written by Dieta-
nitus Willelmi, merchant of Florence, date 1262.
This shows that the Italian form of our name
(Guglielmi) is quite ancient.

In France, the name is not known, and could
not have been in use in olden times, as the French
alphabet originally had no letter "W," though of
late years the latter has been adopted into it, on
account of using English or German names con-
taining that letter. The name *Villaume* is found
in the Biographie Generale, also *Guillaume*, undoubtedly meaning "William."

I found also Willems, (though I believe this
latter was a Hollander), also *Willaumez*, and Wil-
hem, both eminent Frenchman. Some traces of
the name occurs in the archives of Holland. In
Amsterdam records, as early as 1367, is mentioned
one "Claes Dirck, Willems soons son," or grandson
of *Willems*. The name Willems occurs frequently
among the records of the earliest Dutch settlers
in New York, about 1660, and these families subsequently changed their name to the standard
spelling, Williams.

The. Germans have no surname resembling
Williams, whatever. The given name Wilhelm
latinized into Gulielmus) is common, however.
Authors who have written on the etymology of

names have made ludicrous blunders regarding the derivation of "Williams." Arthur says it is derived from the Belgic word *guild-helm*, meaning a golden helmet !

Materials for Genealogical Study.

Common and widely extended as the name is in Great Britain, it is singular that no genealogies of any of the Williams families of that realm have been published. At least the great catalogue of the British Museum shows none, although three genealogies of American families of the name are entered there. Yet some may have been "privately printed" which have not yet been secured by the libraries. "Visitations" in Wales contained pedigrees of the family in a number of cases. I found them in "Glamorganshire Pedigrees (by Sir Isaac Heard), edited by T. Phillipps," published in 1865, and also in Lewis Dunn's "Visitations of Wales," edited by S. R. Meyrick, date 1846. I have advertised in British genealogical serials for a clue to the parentage and descent of "John Williams, ffeltmaker," without result so far, and have also retained the services of two skilled genealogists in Wales to make researches for me and endeavor to secure definite information about our family.

Mr. George E. Clark, a learned antiquary and genealogist of Talygarn, Llantrissant, Wales, to whom I wrote for information, does not seem to regard the chances of my success very highly.

He writes: "I do not think that you will be able, from any records on this side of the water, to establish the descent you undertake. About every tenth man in this part of Wales is called Williams, and about half of these, John Williams. And Welsh pedigrees, though copious, are seldom correct, and very much wanting in dates and places.[1] I am sorry not to be able to promote your very laudable desire."

1. Sir Watkins William Wynne, talking to a friend about the antiquity of his family, which he carried up to Noah, was told that he was a mere mushroom. "Ay!" said he, "how so, pray?" "Why," replied the other, "when I was in Wales a pedigree of a particular family was shown to me; it filled about five large skins of parchment, and about the middle of it was a note in the margin:—'*About this time the world was created!*' "

How Surnames Originated in Wales.

Surnames had not been generally adopted in either Wales or England, much prior to four centuries ago. It was the custom in Wales to designate men by their father's name, to which their own was prefixed. Thus, if a Welshman named "Gwilym" had a son, whose name was also William, the latter would be distinguished by calling him "William ap William," that is, the son of William. Somewhat later on, it would become plain "William Williams." If he had a son named Morgan, the latter would be called Morgan ap Gwilym, or Morgan the son of William. Later on, this would glide into "Morgan Williams." This actually happened in the family of Cromwell, which was Welch, and whose name was originally Williams, as may be learned by reading his life and examining his pedigree there given. It is such a custom as the above which makes the confusion in Welsh pedigrees. Several sons of one family, named Morgan, Evan, Rhys (or Reese), Owen, etc., when the system of surnames was adopted, would thus establish families with the surnames Morgan, Evans, Reese, Owens, etc., and though related in blood, all connection with each other would be lost, in a generation or two.

Gwilym, our Ancestor,

whose name was first given to the extensive and widely spread family now known as "Williams," and who probably flourished in Glamorganshire from 1550 to 1625, must have been a man of considerable means for that period, and of some influence. He was certainly accustomed to arms, and doubtless bore his full share in the troublous wars of his time. When not in the field or camp, he was peacefully employed at home, in the manufacture of hats—a craft of considerable importance at that time. He was doubtless connected by blood, or marriage, with some of the influential families of Glamorganshire, and we hope yet to have his full lineage.

John Williams[1], the Adventurer.

His son, John Williams[1], partook largely of the same characteristics, and grew up into the hereditary handicraft, and with the hereditary love for the saddle and the sword, the fray and the campaign. With a better education than his father, having mixed more largely with the world, and travelled extensively, he set out early in life for a career of adventure and danger. John Williams[1] possessed many admirable traits. He was a staunch Puritan, an honest burgher who feared God but not man—who could pray or fight with equal zest—a brave hater of wrong—a warm advocate of popular rights, and he lived in a period that would call such men into action, too. Events were now occurring which was to change the whole current of his life, and exercise an influence on the destiny of generations of his descendants yet unborn. One of these events was the raising of the fund above spoken of, for the conquest of Ireland. This scheme (which must have warmly enlisted his sympathies) had been begun in the reign of Charles I, but its projectors were delayed in its execution by the civil war, and it does not seem to have been completed until after the overthrow of that monarch and his decapitation in 1669, and it remained for Oliver Cromwell, the Welshman, as Lord Lieutenant, to carry out the conquest of Ireland, and its settlement by his disbanded army and the "adventurers" who had advanced the funds (£43,406) for the military operations. To this fund, John Williams, as mentioned previously, subscribed £50, a very considerable sum for those days, and shows that he must have been a man of some substance. As his name appears to be the 919th on the list, it is probable that he did not subscribe to the adventure until the latter part of the movement, and possibly even after Oliver Cromwell had become identified with it, as the subscription was in progress for several years. This fact, together with the circumstance of John Williams having held the rank of Lieutenant and Commissary in Cromwell's army, during the invasion of Ireland, have led to the assertion on the part of some of the family that he was a cousin of the Protector and also a cousin of Archbishop John Williams, as it is well known that Cromwell descended from a Welch family named Williams, and I have seen that statement made in manuscript genealogies owned by some of our kin. But in the absence of any definite proof of this fact, I can only give it as a "tradition," which will need further genealogical research to substantiate.

When John Williams "the felt maker" went to Ireland in 1649, if that was the year of his emigration, it is probable that he was a man of about forty years of age. It is hardly presumable that he was much if any, less than that age, as, were he a young man, it is not reasonable to suppose that he would have been possessed of means sufficient to have contributed, a sum so considerable, in that period, as £50 to the Irish adventure. It seems quite certain that he was married, and quite probable, also, that he had children, who could not, at that time, have been grown up and consequently must have accompanied him to Ireland, or at least gone there to rejoin him after he received his quota of land in 1653. If so, we have no account of them, thus far, and know only the name of one of his children, John Williams[2], who, we have good grounds to suppose, was born *after* his settlement at "The Groves" and is therefore the first "Irish" Williams, if there is such a personage in our clan.

The Williams Family in Ireland.

O'Hart in his "Irish Pedigrees" states that the soldiers of the commonwealth "were not disbanded, at soonest, before September, 1653, and up to that time they had received no grants of land in Ireland." The same author, in his "Irish and Anglo-Irish Landed Gentry," in the "List of adjudications of arrears of commissioned officers who served before June 5, 1649", gives John Williams' name as one of them. "Lieut. John Williams" is again mentioned as serving as a soldier of the commonwealth, in the county of Louth, and also in "names of persons in the grants under the acts of settlement and explanation." Prendergast states that the act allowing the "adventurers" to cast lots for lands was passed Jan. 1, 1652, but that it was not until "Sept. 26, 1653, that all the ancient estates and farms of the people of Ireland were declared to belong to the Adventurers and the army of England." The "lots" were actually cast in July, 1653. The amount then due the Adventurers was £360,000. Lands in Monaghan County were included in this allotment. It must be remembered that at this time it was deemed very hazardous for the "Adventurers" and others who had been allotted lands under the Cromwellian confiscation, to settle on them. The Irish rebels, who had been forcibly driven from their homes, were infuriated with hatred against the usurpers, and ready for any desperate and bloody act of revenge against the latter. The lands could only be held *vi et armis* by those having a support of soldiery in the vicinity, or a force of workmen and tenantry on their own estates, sufficient to protect themselves from raids, by vigilance and hard fighting. "It was not (says Prendergast) until towards the close of 1653, that the island seemed sufficiently *desolated* (*sic*) to allow the English to occupy it."

Lewis, in his Topographical Dictionary of Ireland, (1860) says of Monaghan County:

"A considerable portion of the lands consists of grants to Cromwell's soldiers, many of whose posterity now possess farms so small as not to yield an annual income exceeding £20. Few of the farms on the larger estates are tenanted in perpetuity. The usual term is 21 years and a life, or 60 years and three lives."

Thus, we find that in 1653, John Williams[1] was most probably put into possession of some 250 acres of land in the county of Monaghan, certainly in the settlement, or neighborhood, now called "the Lower Groves," and "Lappan," 3½ miles due east of the County town of Monaghan, and there established himself as a hat manufacturer and farmer. Here, he must have lived a few years, peacefully, (as we trust) and died, doubtless about 1675, aged probably 70 years. Whether this John Williams[1] built the old stone house which is now in ruins on the "Lower Groves" domain, or not, we cannot now determine. But it is most probable that he did, for it is hardly presumable that the previous dispossessed, Irish rebel tenant, left it there. It is certain, in any event, that John Williams[1] built the addition to the house mentioned elsewhere, which I am positive was for his workshop.

John Williams[2].

An old, broken, and moss-covered tombstone, which I discovered after some search, lying flat in the burying ground attached to Tyholland Church, about 2 miles from "the Groves," gave me the first definite clue to this ancestor. The inscription read: "Here lyeth the body of John Williams, who departed this life Febuary 14th 1723 aged 70 years." This would have made the date of his birth 1653—the year of the supposed settlement of John Williams[1] at the Groves.

And this, so far, is all that we know of John Williams[2]. Was he a son, or a grandson, of John Williams, "ffeltmaker," is a question that may well puzzle us. Further researches among the records may, and probably will, give more full information regarding him and his family. I have conjectured that it may have been this John Williams[2], who is noted on the Parish Records of Tyholland Church, as being a Church warden in said parish, in 1721. There is a well founded legend in the family that he took part in the siege of Londonderry, in 1690 (on the Protestant side of course).

John Williams[3],

Son of the foregoing, was probably born at the Groves, about 1675 or 1680, as, at the time of the Revolution in 1690, he is said to have been about 10 or 15 years old. Whether he had any brothers or sisters, is not now known. His occupation, like that of his father, and grandfather, was that of hatter. He died (so Samuel Williams[6] recorded) "about the age of 75, near the middle of the eighteenth century." From dates given in the Tyholland vestry book, I am inclined to believe that he was living as late as 1754, as he appears to have served as a Church warden in that Parish nearly 30 years. He had nine children, five daughters, and four sons. The names of his daughters or who they married, if they were married, have not been preserved. The sons were named: William, Henry, John and Mathew—though whether in this order, is not known definitely. William and Henry emigrated to America about 1750, and settled in North Carolina. They espoused the royal cause during the revolution, and their property was confiscated. They both died single (at least, so it is supposed).

John Williams[4],

Was born at "the Groves," Dec. 11, 1708. (Another statement says 1714.) He followed the family occupation of hatter. Samuel Williams recorded in his memoirs that "he married (about 1738 or '40) *Sarah* Hall, a most estimable woman by whom he had seven children." But in John Williams'[4] will, (dated 1795) he speaks of his wife as "Elizabeth." It is suggested, however, that the latter was a *second* wife, and not the mother of his children. The wife who bore the latter, must have been a superior woman. Her son, William Williams[5] (my grandfather) always spoke of her in terms of warmest affection, and highest eulogy.

John Williams[4], or his father John Williams[3], acquired the Lappan homestead, which remained in this line for three generations. John Williams[4], is said to have been a strict, severe, exacting man, rigorous in enforcing the tasks given to his children, especially his son, William Williams[5], to whom he taught the hatting business. He was a man of great industry, energy, firmness of will, and more than average intelligence. Some of his marked characteristics have been noticeably impressed on his descendants for three or even four generations. His will, which is a valuable addition to our fund of genealogical data, I fortunately found preserved in the Public Record Office in Dublin. The following is a copy:

In the name of God, Amen. I, John Williams, of Lappan, parish of Tyhallan, and county of Monaghan, being sick of body but of sound and perfect memory, thanks be to God, and calling to mind the uncertainty of this life, do publish and declare this my last will and testament, in manner and form following: first, I leave and bequeath unto my wife, Elizabeth Williams, all the farm of land now in my possession, with my dwelling house and cow house, together with two cows and my mare, my chest of drawers, my bed and bed clothes, and my kitchen furniture, with the following bequests—that at her decease the said houses and land shall go and revert unto John Williams, son to my son Mathew Williams of Lappan aforesaid. Also, I leave unto my said wife all the turf bog I now possess. Also, I leave unto my son William Williams all the land belonging to me, occupied by tenants, if he comes home, and the profits, rents of said lands, until he comes, I leave unto my said wife and said grandson John Williams, equal share and share, and if the said William Williams does not come home before my wife's decease, it is my will that the whole profits of said land go to the said John Williams. Also, I leave unto my son Mathew Williams, my desk. Also, I leave unto my son-in-law, Thomas Short, one shilling, sterling. And it is my will that as soon after my decease as convenient, there shall be an inventory taken of the remainder of my goods and chattels and sold by auction by my executors whom I shall hereafter nominate, and the money arising from the sale thereof, my funeral expenses to be paid thereout, and the remains to be divided equally between my two sons-in-law, viz., William Bell and Thomas Armstrong. And I nominate, constitute and appoint John Williams, of Coot Hill, county of Caven, and William Henderson, of Groves, and county of Monaghan, executors of this my last will and testament.

In witness whereof, I have hereunto put my hand and seal this ninth day of March, 1795.

JOHN WILLIAMS, [Seal].

Signed, sealed, published and declared, in presence of

MATHEW WILLIAMS,

WILLIAM HENDERSON.

1795, July 10, on which day John Williams and William *Anderson*, executors named in the foregoing will, made oath as well to his belief of the truth thereof as also to execute the same.

EDW'D RICE, Com'r.

From this document, which is of great value to us for genealogical purposes, we may infer that John Williams was a well-to-do man for that period, and had quite a good estate. The will was evidently drawn up, and signed by him, while on his death-bed. The signature is a mere scrawl, and evinces the bodily feebleness of the testator. He probably died within a few hours after signing it, aged 87 years. His children were as follows:

Ann Williams 5, born 1747 (?), married William Bell.

William Williams 5, born July 2, 1754, married Margaret Widney.

Mary Williams 5, born 1760 (?), married Thomas Armstrong.

Jane Williams 5, born 1764, (?), married Thomas Short.

Mathew Williams 5, born Feb. 21, 1768, married Margaret Bell.

Elizabeth Williams 5, born 1770 (?), died unmarried [prior to 1795].

One child, died in infancy.

It is not now certain that the names are arranged in the exact order of their birth, but it is believed that they are.

John Williams[4] had 38 grandchildren, and 134 great-grandchildren. Thus he was the progenitor of a mighty line of descendants, all of whom are now living in the United States, and many occupying positions of trust and honor. His son,

William Williams 5,

(grandfather of the writer of this account), was born at Lappan, July 2, 1754. In his youth he received a good education and learned the hatting trade, as an apprentice to his father. About 1779 he married Margaret Widney, of Emyvale,

and lived for several years either at Lappan or
Ballyclareen, a hamlet close by [see map]. In
1783 he appears to have been a churchwarden of
Tyholland parish. Three children were born to
them, all of which died in infancy, the last in
1784, while on their ocean voyage to America.
Mr. Williams settled first in Carlisle, Pa., where
he carried on his trade, then in Path Valley, Pa.,
and in 1803 removed to Charleston, West Virginia,
and in 1807 to Chillicothe, O. Meanwhile three
sons and one daughter were born to him.

Mrs. Margaret (Widney) Williams died at Chillicothe, Dec. 22, 1813, and he himself on August
8, 1815. He was a handsome man, intelligent,
and vivacious in his manners, and a superior
workman at his trade. He had 7 children, 28
grandchildren and 110 great-grandchildren.

La Fabrique de Chapeaux.

The Williamses, for several generations, as
noted above, were hatters by occupation, and
were all superior workmen. They possessed
secrets regarding their craft, with which other
manufacturers were not acquainted, carefully
preserved formulas of their guild, and these were
handed down from father to son for over 150
years. William Williams and his sons also prac-
ticed the calling in America, from 1784 to 1816.
In the choice and combination of materials, in
the fabrication of the stock, in the dyeing and
trimming, and in the shape and style they adopted, the Williamses of the Groves and Lappan were

unsurpassed. Their hats gained a reputation in all that country, and were always in demand. Of course they made all the varieties in vogue in those days—the felt hat, the old fashioned bell-crowned fur hat which every gentleman of position and standing had to wear. They also employed the best workmen to aid them. These doubtless lived in cottages on the estate, as John Williams[4] speaks in his will of his "tenants."

They were in the habit of going to the annual fairs at Ballinsloe, Connaught, and other places, where the best wool was sold, and selecting their supplies at that time. These fairs were the places where they marketed their wares generally, for the selling of goods in stores was not at that time so usual as at the present day. The Williamses were accustomed to visit these fairs with a good stock of hats, the products of the past year's work. The usual mode of transportation in vogue then, was by pack-horses. The wares to be sold were packed in panniers. Their fabrics always went off readily, and they returned with their leathern purses stuffed with the yellow coin of the realm. On one occasion, at one of these fairs, a man stepped up to John Williams and said: "Mr. Williams, here is a hat which I bought of you seven years ago. I should like to get another as good as that." Thus, throughout the region in which their operations were carried on, he had a high reputation, and maintained a large and profitable *clientele* of customers.

The Groves and Lappan—Which is Older?

The question, as to which is the older of the two ancient seats of the Williams family, "the Groves," or "Lappan," may well claim our attention at this point. Family tradition gives the seniority to the Groves homestead as the place where the Williams ancestors planted themselves on coming to Ireland, and I am of the opinion that this is correct, but Wm. Williams, of Dublin, asserts positively that he always heard that Lappan was the first seat of the family. Groves house certainly *seems* the oldest building, in its style and appearance. Just when the Lappan house was built, cannot now be definitely determined, nor by whom. John Williams[2] who died in 1723, was, so the traditions of old people in the neighborhood declare, a resident of the Lappan homestead at the time of his death. Accepting this tradition as correct, I think it is safe to assume that he built it. Why, we are not now informed. The curious question would then come up, had John Williams[1] any other sons, who would have inherited the Groves from him, and kept it, and passed it down the line? John Williams[3] certainly did live at the Groves (according to the parish register) in 1726, and John Williams[4] was born there in 1708 or '14, but more lately was a resident of Lappan, which he certainly occupied some years, and died there, in 1795. His son, William Williams[5], was undoubtedly born at Lappan in 1754. The latter always declared that the

Groves was the original seat of the family. The only solution to the puzzle, is to assume (which I do) that the local tradition that John Williams[2], who was buried in Tyholland churchyard, was of the Lappan house, is an error, and that John Williams[4] was the first one who settled at Lappan and acquired that property either as a gift from his father or by purchase, and built the old Lappan house, or at least the more recent structure. Another inference is, that John Williams[3], of the Groves, the natural heir of John Williams[2], when he died, about 1754, bequeathed the Groves estate to his son Mathew[4], while John[4], for some reason, although the elder, was disinherited, and thereupon went to Lappan, and settled there. But as John Williams[4] was really living at Lappan *prior* to 1754, this somewhat weakens that theory. At any rate, the Lappan house (i. e. the newer portion of it) would date from about the middle of the 18th century at least. Its ancient appearance now, would warrant fixing to it a date certainly as remote as that. Another theory is, that the Groves and Lappan estates were formerly one, and divided between the two sons of the family, John[4] and Mathew[4]. I am more inclined to accept this supposition than any other. The two houses are just half a mile apart, in an air line. Still, presuming that the original "Adventurer," John Williams[1], the ffeltmaker, did receive in the original allotment of land by Cromwell, 250 acres, it could be possible that the boundaries of said tract included both the "Groves" and "Lappan" property. A half mile square, as is well known, amounts to 160 acres.

The Groves Line.

However this may be, we do know beyond a doubt that, about the middle of the 18th century, the Williamses were inhabiting both the Groves and Lappan homesteads, and carrying on the manufacture of hats and farming. Let us now follow, for a moment, the fortunes of the Groves branch.

Mathew Williams [4], son of John Williams [3] and —— ——, was born at the Groves, perhaps about 1730. He married Anne Smith, of Coote Hill, perhaps about 1755. The latter died March 27, 1781, aged 44 years. Her tomb is in Tyholland churchyard. His body was subsequently buried in the same grave. The children of Mathew [4] and Anne (Smith) Williams were as follows:

Alexander Willams [5], born (a) 1760, married Eliza Bocock.
John Williams [5], married —— ——, died Jan. 10, 1808.
William Williams [5], unmarried, died April 2, 1810.
Mathew Williams [5], married Mary Thompson.
Sally Williams [5], married Woodney Browne.
Margaret Williams [5], married Matthew Browne.
Elizabeth Williams [5], died unmarried, by her own act.

Mathew Williams [4], probably died about the close of the 18th century, aged about 70 or 75 years. His eldest son, Alexander Williams [5], in the natural operation of the law of primogeniture, should have inherited from him the Groves estate. He was an industrious and energetic young man. But in some way, perhaps through the influence of relatives, Mathew Williams[4] was induced to bequeath the homestead to Mathew Williams[5], a younger son. Finding himself disinherited of what he had always deemed was his rightful patrimony, Alexander Williams[5] left his father's house, to fight his own battle with fortune, with a heart full of bitterness at the supposed scheming which had supplanted him in his birth-right. Pausing after he left the old house, in the beautiful alley lined with hawthorns, and looking around, from that lovely eminence, over the fertile paternal acres which had slipped from his grasp, the natural and excusable feelings of his heart overcame him, and he raised his hand, exclaiming, "the curse of God be upon the house." When I stood and looked at the ruins of the old homestead three-quarters of a century later, and thought of that imprecation, it almost seemed that the wild and thoughtless prayer of the young man had been answered. But Alexander Williams was not of the stuff that yields tamely to reverses. He went to Dublin and became a successful man, raising a fine family, and died in 1843, universally respected.

A Tragic Event at the Groves.

Ordinarily, life in that lovely rural spot, must have flowed on quietly and calmly, unbroken by rude shocks, or sudden reverses of fortune. Generations were born into the old house, and their cold still forms were in time borne out of it, to the ancient churchyard at Tyholland. But once there occurred such a tragedy there, that traditions of it are current at this day in the neighborhood. Elizabeth Williams[5] was the youngest daughter of Mathew Williams[4]. She was born about 1780, and about the beginning of the present century was just developing into a lovely womanhood. She was a charming and affectionate maiden, and the favorite of the family. She had bestowed her love, and promised her hand, on a suitor in the neighborhood, but for some reason not now remembered, she had been disappointed in her expectations, and the match was broken off. Of a sensitive and tender nature, this blighting of her affection affected her very severely and resulted in melancholy depression and temporary dementia. One evening while she was setting the table for tea, the thought of her disappointment probably agitated her more uncontrollably than usual, and without saying a word to anybody, she slipped out of the house, and runing to the well a few feet down the slope, threw herself in. Her absence was noticed in a short time, and search being made, the body of the unfortunate girl was found in the water entirely lifeless. The sorrow of the family can better be imagined than described. The old well was filled up, and a new one opened a little distance below it. The location of the first one is still to be recognized.

Further Legends About The Old Groves House.

Among a people as superstitious as the rural population of Ireland was at that time, it was easy for any foolish story of anything supernatural, to gain full credence. Though they were not spiritualists (for "spiritualism" was not known at that time), yet the simple country folks readily credited any absurd "ghost story." And this is how the rumor spread, that the spirit of the poor girl whose life had so tragically ended, came back to visit her former residence. There were strange stories of ghostly visitations at the old house. How two young men, sons of Mathew Williams[4], sleeping in the bedroom at the north end of the old house, heard mysterious footsteps on the floor. And occasionally heavy objects, apparently, would be thrown on the table and the floor, which would almost make the timbers vibrate, and shake their bed; but no traces or marks of these demonstrations remained at daylight. Yet, thus, little by little, the legend grew that the old manse was haunted. And when, a few years subsequently, the Williams clan entirely abandoned the old homestead (for Mathew Williams[5] did not retain possession of it long), it was difficult to get a tenant to live there, and little by little it became permanently empty, then was abandoned to baser uses—a stable— then a desolate ruin.

The Groves and Lappan in 1888.

For many years, the writer of this sketch, had resolved to make a pilgrimage to the ancient homesteads of the family in the county of Monaghan, and ascertain what facts he could, regarding the history of the Williamses of Monaghan clan. It was not until 1888, when I was able to accomplish this, in connection with a general European tour, at the close of which, in the month of September, I visited Neath and Cadoxton, Wales, the ancient Cymbrian home of the Gwilym tribe, and from thence proceeded to Dublin, Ireland, where (on September 13), I received a warm Irish welcome from our cousins William[6] and James[6] Williams, and their families. Mr. Wm. Williams[6], No. 2, Dame St, is a naturalist by profession, a gentleman of fine attainments and much scientific knowledge, and author of valuable treatises on natural history. Mr. James Williams[6] resides at No. 43, Dame St. Although suffering somewhat from the infirmities of age, Mr. Wm. Willams[6] kindly offered to accompany me to the old family home, and it was fortunate that he did so, as his knowledge of the localities, and of the family history, were of the very greatest value to me. We arrived at Monaghan on Friday evening, September 14, and were cordially greeted by Mr. Robert Whitla, brotherinlaw of Wm. Williams[6], who took us to his comfortable residence, where his amiable wife, formerly Miss Anne Williams[6], and daughter, Maggie, soon made their "American cousin" feel perfectly at home, and I passed an evening of delightful social intercourse with these excellent people.

The next morning (September 15), which we had planned to employ in visiting the Groves and Lappan, was cold and rainy. Cousin Wm. Williams[6] was feeling too unwell to venture out in such weather, but as my time in Ireland was so limited, I felt that I could not lose an hour. Wrapping myself up in my water-proof ulster, I at once sought a livery stable, and hired a "jaunting car," with a smart driver, and a brisk nag, and started off to visit

Emyvale,

An old town five miles north of Monaghan, where the Widney family lived over a century ago, and where my grandfather, William Williams[5], wedded Margaret Widney just a century ago. The roads were splendid, smooth and hard, and we galloped along between the beautiful hedges of hawthorn, through rows of century old trees that lined the highway, past comfortable stone houses, along carefully cultivated fields, and all this through a landscape of incomparable loveliness. Soon the rain ceased and the clouds broke away. We reached Emyvale in about an hour. It is a quaint old Irish town, built along the highway for over half a mile. All the houses are one-story stone structures, many of them very poor, with thatched roof, and it is certain, from their appearance, that not a new house had been built in the town for a

century, at least. The people generally seemed
very poor. Perhaps the number of signs that I
noticed over doors, "Licensed to sell spirits," may
account partly for this. I went into several
dwellings and stores, and was pained at the appearance of poverty and discomfort everywhere.
My main object in visiting Emyvale, was to get
some trace of the Widney family. To this end, I
conversed with several very old people, one, in-
deed, who said he could remember back eighty
years, but I could find no one who had heard the
the name Widney. I enquired of the postmistress
also, but she asserted that there was no such
name ever enquired for at her office, so I abandoned further search, and started off to find the
rector of Glaslough church, in which church I felt
certain that the marriage of William Williams[5]
and Margaret Widney must have taken place.
Glaslough itself is a village some two miles from
Emyvale, and the residence of the rector is on the
road between the two places. As I rode along, I
could vividly picture to myself the scene of a
century and more ago, when "Billy Williams," of
Lappan, a handsome young fellow of about twen-
ty-five, dressed in knee breeches, and wearing
one of the best hats made in his father's shop
(perhaps made by his own hands), walked along
this same highway, through the fragrant hawthorn hedges, on Saturday evenings, on his way
to court the handsome Maggie Widney, or to es-
cort her to a country ball. We soon reached

Glaslough rectory, a beautiful villa embowered in an old forest, and I alighted and enquired for the rector, Rev. J. C. Hudson. Unfortunately, he was absent from home, so I was baffled in my project of examining the Donagh parish registers of a century ago. I subsequently found by corresponding with him, that the parish had no registers earlier than 1836, all prior to that date havbeen lost or destroyed. We were now in the immediate vicinity of Cool-Collet-hill, where was the old homestead of the Anderson family, but I did not have time to visit it, to my great regret.

We returned to Monaghan, and the weather having now become warm and clear, cousin William Williams[6] and I, set off after dinner in a car, to visit

The Groves and Monaghan.

These ancient seats of our clan are situated about three and one-half miles directly east from Monaghan, on the grand highway to Armagh. We soon passed the Ballyclareen river, a stream in which the Williams boys used to fish, generation after generation, and a few steps beyond, hailed an old native making hay by the roadside, of whom Wm. Williams[6] inquired which was the Lappan house. "Is it the ould Williams house ye want?" said the rustic. "Its yon," pointing to a structure on an eminence near by. This was, for us, an interesting incident. The Williams family had not occupied either of their old homesteads in this locality for over a half century, and yet here was a local tradition calling the old houses by the names of their ancient proprietors. Thus tenacious of life are local traditions in that region.

On reaching the top of the hill, we saw the Lappan house on our left, up a long lane, and the ruins of the Groves house, plainly in sight, half a mile distant, on an eminence, across a low valley. We determined to visit this first, and drove thither. Just as we turned off from the highway into the hawthorn-hedged lane that led to the old ancestral manse, we were fortunate enough to meet a clever farmer who lived close by, Mr. Samuel Gilliland, who greeted us politely and asked us if we were Williamses? On replying "yes," he said he had suspected it from our personal appearance, and that the idea came to him who we were, and our object, when he saw our car approaching the old place. He was very glad to see us, and offered to show us the Groves house, or what remains of it, with which he had been familiar since childhood, and it was lucky for us that we met him as we did, as he gave me much very valuable and interesting information.

The Old "Groves" House.

As I dismounted from the car, at the site of the old house, on the summit of the eminence, a painful feeling came over me, as I saw its ruinous condition. I would have given a large sum to have seen it as it was when whole and in good order, such as our ancestors inhabited a century or two ago.

Still, enough of its walls remain, to show what
it was, and its arrangement and appearance. Mr.
Gilliland kindly explained to me the interior
arrangement and appearance, as he had been in
it hundreds of times when a boy, and remem-

THE "GROVES:

bered nearly all the particulars regarding it.
With his aid, and my own measurements, I drew
a plan of the house, which he pronounced correct.
I also made a pencil sketch of the ruins, which
is herein copied by the photo engraving process.
The house was probably 40 feet front, and 24
deep. It was well and thoroughly built of hewn
stone, and had been stuccoed both outside and inside. It was 1½ stories high, and had (as do all
the houses in that region), a thatched roof. Mr.
Gilliland says it was a well finished and comfortable residence and looked very neat on the outside. To the north of the main house, was an addition quite spacious in size, one story in height,
which, I have no doubt, was used for the hat

shop.   Still north of this, down the slope, a little,
and detached from the house, was a large barn,
built of stone, which is still standing in good con-

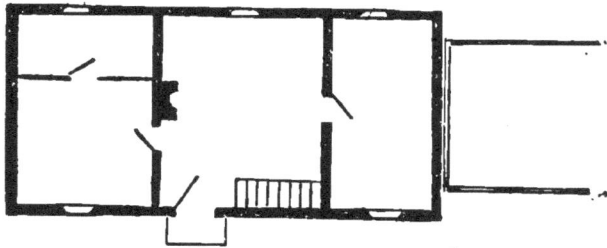

CROVES - Ground Plan.

dition.   Wm. Williams[6] asserts that his grand-·
father, Mathew Williams[4], built this.   The second floor of this barn, when not occupied by
grain, or other products, was used for a ball room,
and was very suitable for that purpose.   Here
the country beaux and belles used to tread the
rustic dances, set in motion by some rural fiddlers,
and the rafters of the old structure have doubtless resounded many a time with the musical
laughter of the buxom Irish lasses, and their
brawny laddies.

Adown the slope, toward the west, a few feet,
was once the ill-fated well in which Elizabeth
Williams[5] ended her young life.   Fruit trees were
scattered around the house, and along the front
wall of the yard.   Farther on, was the vegetable
garden.   The main cultivated fields, were on the
east side of the lane.   West of the house, in the
valley, was an immense peat bog, over a mile

long, in which the family got their fuel for over a century. It is now exhausted, and turned into a meadow, carpeted with bright verdure.

The Groves house stands on a lovely eminence. The name Monaghan is said to signify, "the little hills," and this describes the appearance of the country—a succession of undulations as far as the eye can reach. Standing on the ground by the Groves house, one can see two or three miles in every direction, a most lovely panorama of green fields, cultivated patches, just then yellow for the harvest, with lines of deep green hedges around the fields, stone walls, clumps of trees and white-washed stone cottages. I have never laid eyes on a more charming landscape. The sight of the old homestead revived some interesting reminis-cences in William Williams, about the family's life there, that I wish I had room to insert in this sketch. One incident shows how attached the family were to the old place. William Williams was once returning to the Groves with Sallie (Williams) Browne, who had been absent from home sometime. On reaching the hawthorn hedge that bordered the old lane, and recognizing the old roof-tree, she was so overcome by the memories of her happy days of childhood con-nected with the familiar spot, that she burst into tears.

The soil of the Groves neighborhood is as rich and productive as any I ever saw anywhere. I wish some descendant of the family would purchase

the property, which is now for sale, and rebuild
the old house, as a memorial to our ancestors.

A Visit to Lappan.

After lingering around the old place as long as
we could, we bade good bye to neighbor Gilliland,
and mounted our car, to pay a visit to Lappan.
In order to show the relative position of the
Groves and Lappan, I give here a map, copied
from the Ordnance Survey of Great Britain.

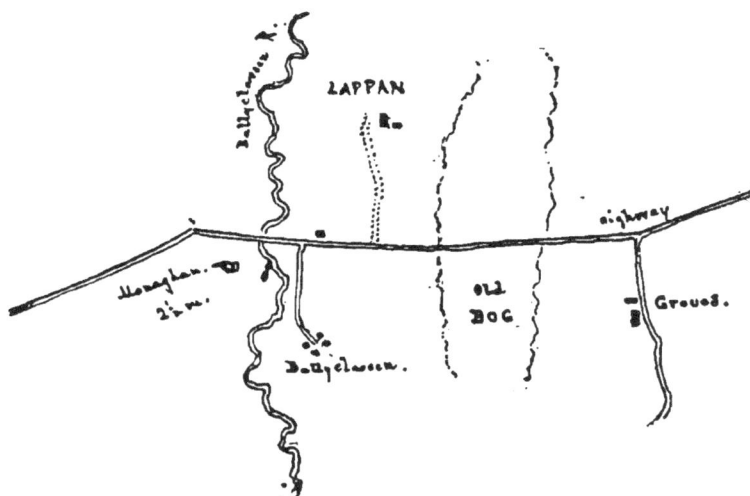

In a few moments we were driving up the hedged
lane of the Lappan estate. Mr. James Hughes,
the present tenant of the farm, advanced to meet
us. He had already suspected who we were and
our purpose, and when we alighted remarked, "I
think your names are Williams?" Guided by
him, we commenced an inspection of the premi-
ses, to me a most interesting spot. We appeared

to approach the old house in the rear, a fact which
Mr. Hughes explained by stating that the house
had once fronted to the east on a roadway that
then ran north and south on the other side of it,
but which had since been closed up and was
now cultivated ground. On my Ordinance survey map, dated 1836, I find that the road did
then run east of the house, as he said.

The house, like all those in this region, was of
stone, a story and a half high, and covered with
a thatched roof. It was stuccoed on the outside,
and brilliantly whitewashed. It was a neat looking residence outwardly, but showed marks of
antiquity. It was probably 50 feet front, and 24
deep.

I entered this venerable house of our ancestors
through the low doorway, with feelings such as
became the occasion, and sat down in the main
family room. Inside it was poorly lighted, and
the rafters and ceiling above were absolutely
ebonized by the smoke from the fireplace where
peat had been burned for 150 years, and by lamp
smoke, etc. A woman was leaning over the fireplace, cooking, probably,—a woman with some
traces of intelligence and beauty, but showing
the marks of hard work and hopeless poverty.
There was no wooden floor in the entire house,
and perhaps there never had been one. The floor
was paved with stone and brick, and it appeared
very old and much worn. It was undoubtedly
the one which was put down when the house was

built.   An old staircase, not enclosed, ran from
the rear of the room, to the attic above. It looked
more ancient than anything else; the oaken
planks seemed worn hollow by the footsteps of
a century and a half.   The walls were roughly
plastered, and had been white once.   The doors
and their frames, the windows and window frames,
were all very old and battered, and showed the
marks of wear and time.   There were two quite
large apartments in the house, and two smaller
ones.   Accompanying is a plan:

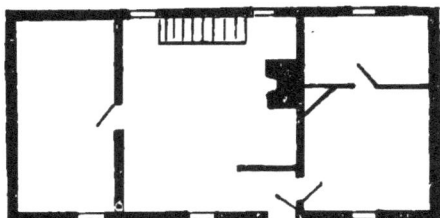

LAPPAN — GROUND PLAN.

Running at right angles to the house, was a
rough stone structure, used now as a stable.   It
may have once been the hatting shop, but Wm.
Williams thinks this was the original dwelling of
the family, and that the other building was
erected subsequently.   We cannot fix the date of
either definitely. In his will (1795) John Williams[4]
evidently refers to it as the "cow house," which I
think it always was.   A stone wall ran in front of
this, the ancient enclosure along the line of the
once road, above referred to.   In front of this the

ground slopes off to the eastward, towards the peat bog mentioned in the will of John Williams[4] who died in the Lappan house in 1795. The peat has long ago all been cut off from it, and it is now meadow land. It is underlaid by a splendid bed of marl, from which the best quality of bricks are now made.

Mr. Hughes is an industrious and intelligent man, but speaks of his condition and prospects very despondingly. He says he has to work very hard, early and late, for a very poor living, and cannot get ahead. He pays £13 a year rent for his land, of which he has ten acres. This, he says, is the general condition of all the small Irish farmers. The land he rents now belongs to the Coote Estate, descendants of the Earl of Bellomont at Coote Hill, County Cavan. The land, however, is very rich and productive.

I remained at Lappan, walking about, and carefully examining it, until evening, when the hour came to return to the city. I left this interesting neighborhood, the Groves and Lappan, with much regret, and with many emotions as I thought of their past, and the fortunes of the family identified with them. I hope to see them again.

Some Historical Notes on Ancient Monaghan.

The region in which Monaghan is included, was the home of the Irish tribes since remote ages. In the "allotment of 1591" the Groves fell to Toole McGilduffe MacMahon, and Lappan to Con

O'Clerian. After the conquest of Ireland by Cromwell, 1649, the country was reapportioned. An ancient map of Ulster, fully 300 years old, with letter press description in Latin, gives the following account of Monaghan:

Erno lacui ad orientem praetenditur Mouaghan, Comitatus collibus, aditus, sylvis vestitus, sed nullo notus oppido, nisi Monaghan, quod nomen universo agro impertiit, dividitur in quinque baronias, etc.

Skirting Lake Ernus on the east lies Monaghan, hilly, elevated, covered with forests, marked by no town except Monaghan. which name is shared by the whole region. It is divided into five baronies, etc.

"The Groves" must have been so called from the ancient forests which once covered that neighborhood, and are spoken of in the foregoing extract and by other early writers, as very heavy and extensive. Nothing remains of them now.

The word "Lappan," says Evelyn Philip Shirley in his history of Monaghan county, signifies, in the Irish tongue, "a little paw." The name is evidently a very ancient one.

According to the Ordinance Survey, Lappan now has 102 acres, and the Groves (lower) 117. The Groves (upper), I am told by a person residing there, was once part of the possessions of the Williams family, and must have been sold by them a long time ago, as the dwelling house on it, occupied by a Mrs. Patten, seems very old. This is some quarter of a mile south of the old Groves house.

A Visit to Tyholland Church.

The next day (Sept. 16) was the Sabbath, and I resolved to pay a visit to Tyholland church, to see that venerable structure, in which our ancestors worshipped for over 150 years, and in the yard of which, I had reason to believe, some of them were buried.* Cousin Maggie Whitla[7] kindly offered to accompany me, and engaging a car, we reached Tyholland church a few minutes before the time for service, 12 o'clock. The day was a lovely one.

I went at once to the burial ground, accompanied by Miss Whitla, and commenced my search, although the bell for service was even then ringing. I found, without delay, the tomb of Mrs. Anne Williams, since we knew where it was. I then continued my investigations. After reading the inscriptions on a number of grave stones, I noticed one very ancient looking one, lying flat, and covered with dirt, moss, grass, etc. I scraped some of this away with my foot, and read the letters WIL. This made me believe I had found that of one of our family, and I at once eagerly began to pry it up and scrape off the dirt from it.

Just then the church bell ceased to toll, and I was compelled to suspend my search and go in to service. We asked one of the vestrymen if he could show us into the old pew known as the

---

* Tyholland is a very ancient locality. Its name dates back to 1306, when it was called Tech-thalain, or Tech-talam, "House of Talan," subsequently spelled Tehallan, and now Tyholland. St. Patrick is said to have founded the original church. The present building (on the site of the ancient one) is about 200 years old.

"Williams pew," which he did. The family undoubtedly worshipped in this pew over a century. The interior of Tyholland church is quite plain, but there is a movement on foot to restore it. The pews are the old fashioned square ones. where a part of the audience sit with their back to the desk. The backs of the pews were straight, the seats uncushioned, and not very comfortable or easy. I remembered my own dreary hours when a child, seated on like benches, and regarding it all as a sort of punishment, and thought, with sympathy, of the Williams boys of Lappan and Groves, with their little feet swinging several inches from the floor, seated wearisomely on these same benches, and trying hard to keep still. But it did not give them a hatred to religion, as they all became good Christians, in time.

When the services were closed, I sought the rector, Rev. James Wilson, whom I found to be a very courteous and affable gentleman. I told him my errand to Tyholland, and he assured me he would aid me in any way he could. He, accompanied by his wife and two sons, went with me to the old stone I had found in the yard, and I went to work on it again. aided by the sexton, who brought a broom and a pail of water, with which we cleansed the surface of the stone. Quite a group gathered around, much interested in the proceedings. At length I was able to read the inscription on it as follows:

HERE LYETH THE
BODY OF IOHN
WILLIAMS WHO DEPA
RTED THIS LIFE FEBUARY
THE 14TH 1723 AGED 70 YEARS.

I felt a great joy when I had deciphered this, as it convinced me that I was on the right track, and I had now got a definite clue, after all my outlay and trouble. I was not able, however, to continue my researches then, as the hour was already late. We accepted the kind invitation of Mr. and Mrs. Wilson to accompany them to the rectory a few steps distant, where we partook of · refreshments, and then returned to the city on foot. That evening I left for Belfast where I was hospitably entertained by Dr. William Whitla[7] and his wife, and the next day returned to Dublin, en route for Queenstown, where I was to embark on the steamer.

Believing that there were other old tombstones of the earlier members of our family still to be found at Tyholland, I enlisted Dr. William Whitla[7], of Belfast, in the project to have the place thoroughly examined. He caused this to be done soon after, by a competent person, but no more tombstones of our family were found. This was somewhat of a disappointment to me, as I was certain that more would be discovered, which would give us valuable facts and dates. Still, the decayed condition of the tombstone of John Williams[2] that I found, leads me to believe that the others may have crumbled to pieces.

The Williamses as Churchmen.

From the vestry book of Tyholland Parish, which records reach back to the year 1712, we learn that the Williamses were all devoted members of the Established Church, and that several of them held offices in the Parish during more than a century of its history. Rev. James Wilson, Rector, has copied for me a number of extracts from the old vestry book, which are very valuable to us, as giving much light on the history of the family. John Williams, "of Groves," appears to have been elected Church warden at various times, from 1721 to 1771, and most probably served continuously during all that period. The minutes which refer to him as such, are dated Jan. 2, 1721; Apr. 12, 1726; Apr. 5, 1743; Mar. 27, 1751; Apr. 15, 1754; Apr. 10, 1770, and Oct. 1, 1771. I must confess that I am somewhat puzzled to determine whether it is the same John Williams, or not, that is referred to in all these entries. I had started out on the theory that it was John Williams[3], "of Groves," born in 1675 (perhaps) and, who in 1721, when he is first noted as a Church warden, would have been 46 years old. But the first entry noted, may relate to John Williams[2], who did not die until Feb. 14, 1723. It could not certainly have been John[4], because he was not born until 1708 (some accounts say 1714). In two entries, the person referred to is termed "John Williams, of Groves." These are on Apr. 12, 1726, and on Apr. 15, 1754. But we have been led to

believe that John Williams[3] died about 1750. Yet
it may have been he who is noted on the records
even as late as 1754, for he may have lived until
after that date. It could not certainly have been
John[3], who was the Church warden in 1771; no
residence of this one is mentioned on the records.
I am rather inclined to believe that this latter
was John[4], who at that date (1771) had become
the proprietor of Lappan, and who died there in
1795, and whose will is given in a previous portion
of this work. The other entries in the Tyholland
Parish Record, are as follows:

Apr. 15, 1754, William Bell, (son-in-law of John Williams[4]) mentioned as vestryman.

Apr. 16, 1759, Walter Bell, mentioned as Church warden, and
Mathew Williams as a vestryman.

Apr. 10, 1770, John Williams, mentioned as Church warden.

Oct. 1, 1771, John Williams, mentioned as Church warden, and
Mathew Williams, as a vestryman.

Apr. 21, 1783, Wm. Williams, of Bally Clareen,* as Church
warden.

Apr. 6, 1795, Alexander Williams, of Groves, Church warden.

Nov. 27, 1824, Mathew Williams, signs as an officer.

Thus it will be seen, that for over a century,
the heads of the various families of Williams, in
Tyholland Parish, during three generations, if not
four, were prominent as Church officers in that
Parish. Only men well to do, living under the
tongue of good repute, and leading blameless
lives, were chosen to those offices. I regret that
their descendants did not more generally adhere
to the Church of their ancestors. Most of them
have gone after strange Gods. I think that the

*Bally Clareen is a hamlet about one-third mile south of Lappan.

Richmond, Va., Williamses are about the only families who have followed the faith of their fathers, and we should honor them for it.

It is gratifying to know that our ancestors were devout and pious people. The influence of heredity is very powerful. *"Bon sang ne peut mentir."* Good progenitors generally have good descendants, and their best traits are thus perpetuated from generation to generation. All the Williamses that I have ever heard of, are religious people, many of them intensely so. I do not believe that there is a skeptic or atheist in the entire sept, or ever was.

Some Ethnological Notes.

During their residence in Ireland of about a century, (or more, in some lines), the Williamses do not seem to have intermarried with the native race, at all. This may have been largely owing to differences in religion, nationality, or social position.

The Wilsons were Scotch; Hall is a Scotch name, (also Welsh). The Widneys were of Hollandish descent. Bell is Scotch, and so is Armstrong, Anderson, Johnston, McAllister, McCullough, Browne, Campbell, Linn, Gordon, and other families noted herein, who have married with the Williams Clan. So that the Williams Family would appear to be almost entirely and purely Welsh-Scotch, in blood. Their general physical characteristics and temperaments also indicate Celtic (Cymbrian) Origin.

I have now traced the history of our family for nearly 300 years, out of their ancient dwelling place among the mountains of Wales, into the verdant slopes of Ireland, and thence, after a century's tarrying, to that grandest and most favored of all lands, America.

I regret that my time while in Ireland was so limited. My return ocean passage had been engaged, and I was obliged to sail on September 19th.

There are other records in Ireland, of whose existence I did not learn until I was about to leave, which would undoubtedly give us many valuable facts of family history. I hope that some younger member of our tribe will pursue the investigations, along the lines I have indicated.

The absence of any family manuscripts or papers, such as letters, wills, deeds, records in family bibles, etc., was another cause which added much to my labors, and to their unfruitfulness. None of the branches of our family seem to have any of these records which reach back any distance, and the loss of all the oldest parish registers has destroyed valuable data of that kind.

Conclusion.

I now leave to some other hands the completion of our genealogical history. I trust that some one, with ample means and leisure, and a genuine fondness for the work, will take it up and complete the tree, collecting the name of every person who can trace his or her lineage back to "John Williams, ffelt-maker." It will require some very patient person, too, as he will find a discouraging indifferenceon the part of many to whom he applies for facts. Many letters which I wrote to members of the family for information, did not receive the courtesy of an acknowledgment. But I trust that the publication of this brochure may tend to increase the interest in the family, regarding its history. One other point that I wish to allude to is the importance of keeping in every family some accurate records of births, marriages and deaths. Some families to whom I sent for information, had no written records of this kind, whatever, and were compelled to guess at dates. A good plan to accomplish this registry, would be, for persons receiving this volume to have it bound, adding to it a number of leaves of writing paper, on which to record such genealogical facts as they deem valuable for preservation.

In order to aid in such a commendable work, and to give each member of the family now living a clue to connect his descent back to the earliest known progenitors of the family, I append a pedigree, not complete in all portions, and only including the first seven generations, but which will, nevertheless, be found useful, as it is the first time our family record has been put into print.

It is arranged in the form and style now used by the most skilled genealogists, and is very simple and easily understood. To have extended it through the eighth and ninth generations (and possibly the tenth has now begun to appear on the stage, at least on this side of the water), would have delayed this publication too long.

THE LINEAGE OF WILLIAMS.

1. John Williams,[1]

Called the "ffeltmaker." Born in Glamorganshire, Wales, about 1600. Emigrated to Ireland about 1649 and settled at "the Groves, Monaghan County, 1653. Date of death, and name of wife, unknown.

2. John Williams[2],

Son of foregoing, (but may have been a grandson). Born, probably at the Groves, 1653. Died, do, Feb. 14, 1723. His tombstone is in Tyholland church yard. He took part in the Siege of Londonderry. Name of wife, unknown.

3. John Williams[3].

Son of foregoing. Born at the Groves about 1680. Died, do, about 1755. Name of wife unknown. He had four sons and tive daughters. The names of the latter are unknown. His sons were :

    i. William Williams[4]. Emigrated to North Carolina, and died single.

    ii. Henry Williams[4]. Emigrated to North Carolina, and died single.

4. iii. John Williams[4]. Born at the Groves, Dec. 11, 1708 [1714?] Died at Lappan, March, 1795.

5. iv. Mathew Williams[4]. Born at the Groves, a. 1720. Died do, a. 1798.

    v-ix. Five daughters, names unknown.

4. John Williams[4],

Son of John Williams[3]. Born at the Groves Dec. 11, 1708 [1714?] Died at Lappan March, 1795. His will is on record in Dublin. Married 1. Sarah Hall; 2. Elizabeth ——, and had issue by his first wife:

6.   i.   Ann Williams[5], b. 1747. Married Wm. Bell.

7.   ii. William Williams [5], b. July 2, 1754. Married Married Margaret Widney.

8. iii. Mary Williams[5], b. 1760. Married Thomas Armstrong.
9   iv. Jane Williams[5], b. 1764, Married Thomas Short.
10   v. Mathew Williams , b. Feb. 20, 1768. Married Margaret Bell.
     vi. Elizabeth Williams[5], b. 1770. Died unmarried.

5. Mathew Williams,[4]

Son of John Williams[3], and ——————. Born at the Groves about 1720. Died at same place about 1798. Married Ann Smith, and had issue:

11. i. Alexander Williams[5], b. about 1760. Married Eliza Bocock.
12. ii. John Williams[5], of Coote Hill. Married——————. Died at Lappan, Jan. 10, 1808.
     iii. William Williams[5]. Died unmarried, Apr. 2, 1810.
13. iv. Mathew Williams[5], b. at the Groves, 1773. Married Mary Thompson.
14. v. Sally Williams[5], b. at the Groves about 1775. Married Woodney Browne.
15. vi. Margaret Williams[5], b. at the Groves about 1777. Married Mathew Browne.
     vii. Elizabeth Williams[5], b. at the Groves about 1780. Died unmarried, by her own act.

6. Ann Williams[5],

Eldest daughter of John Williams[4] and Sarah Hall, born at Groves, Monaghan Co., Ireland, about 1747; died, 1808, in Pennsylvania. She married Wm. Bell, and had:

16. i. Sarah Bell[6], b. 1769. Married James Anderson.
     ii. Rachel Bell[6], b. 1771. Married Thomas Hoy. They had 13 children, of which we have no account.
     iii. Walter Bell[6], b. July 24, 1775. Died June 18, 1849.
     iv. John Bell[6], b. 1778. Died Aug. 17, 1802.
17. v. William Bell[6], b. Feb. 11, 1781. Married Margaret V. Dwight.
18. vi. Samuel Bell[6], b. 1784. Died 1842.
19. vii. Ann Bell[6], b. 1786. Married C. S. Semple.
20. viii. Elizabeth Bell[6], b. 1789. Married John Buchanan, etc.
     ix. David Bell[6], b. 1793. Married Elizabeth Owen. No issue.
     x. Mary Bell[6], b. 1794. Died unmarried in 1818.

7. William Williams[5],

Son of John Williams[4] and Sarah Hall. Born at Lappan, July 2, 1754. Married, 1779, Margaret Widney, of Emyvale. Emigrated to Pennsylvania, 1784. He died at Chillicothe, O., 1815; she in 1813. They had:

Three sons died in infancy.

21. i. Samuel Williams[6], b. Oct. 16, 1786. Married: 1. Eliza Armstrong; 2. Margaret Troutner.

22. ii. George Young Williams[6], b. Oct. 11, 1788. Married Mary Thompson.

23. iii. Mary Ann Williams[6], b. Oct. 15, 1792. Married Wm. Bailey.

24. iv. William Williams[6], b. Nov. 14, 1794. Married: 1. Elizabeth Bayless. 2. Maria C. Buckingham.

8. Mary Williams[5],

Daughter of John Williams[4] and Sarah Hall. Born at Lappan, Monaghan County, Ireland, 1760. Died Feb, 4, 1809, in Pennsylvania. Married Thomas Armstrong. Had issue:

i. Sally Armstrong[6], b. 1773. Died single.

ii, Catherine Armstrong[6], b. 1775. Married Robert Blackburn.

25. iii. Jane Armstrong[6], b.—— (?). Married James Campbell.

26. iv. John Armstrong[6], b. 1779. Married Rebecca Rule.

27. v. Eliza Armstrong[6], b. July, 1785. Married Samuel Williams (No. 21).

vi. Hugh Armstrong[6], b. —— (?). Died unmarried.

vii. Ann Armstrong[6], b. —— (?). Married Jacob Aid.

viii. William Armstrong[6], b. ——. Died unmarried.

9. Jane Williams[5],

Daughter of John Williams[4] and Sarah Hall. Born at Lappan, Monaghan County, Ireland, 1764. Married Thomas Short. Had issue:

i. James Short[6]. Settled in Fairfield County, Ohio.

ii. Elizabeth Short[6]. Married Wm. Beck, and settled in Dublin.

Mrs. Jane (Williams) Short, after the death of Mr. Short, married —— Graham and lived in Dublin.

10. Mathew Williams[5],

Son of John Williams[4] and Sarah Hall. Was born at Lappan, Monaghan County, Ireland, Feb. 28, 1768, and died July 30, 1835. He married Margaret Bell. She died Aug. 28, 1840, in the U. S. Had issue:

28.   i.   John Williams[6], b. March 26, 1793. Married Sianna A. Dandridge.

        ii.   William Williams[6]. Married Ann Greenhow.

28½ iii.   Thomas G. Williams[6]. Married Frances Greenhow.

        iv.   Sarah Williams[6]. Married Mathew Johnson.

        v.   Walter Williams[6]. Born Oct. 1, 1800, d Dec. 30, 1837.

        vi.   Anne Williams[6]. Born 1802. Married Robert Johnson.

29. vii.   Mathew B. Williams[6]. Born Dec. 9, 1805. Married Margaret McAllister.

        viii.   David Williams[6]. Born Dec. 16, 1808, d. Sept. 26, 1839.

        ix.   Henry Williams[6]. Born 1800, d. April 15, 1832.

        x.   Alfred Williams[6]. Born 1814, d. March 11, 1831.

        xi.   Margaret Williams[6]. Married ——— Crozier.

11. Alexander Williams[5],

Son of Mathew Williams[4] and Ann Smith. Born at the Groves about 1770. Married Eliza Bocock about 1800. He died 1843, and is buried in Monaghan. Had issue:

30.   i.   John Alexander Williams[6]. Born Manchester, Eng., about 1805. Married Alice Pierson, London.

        ii.   Alexander[2], ⎱
                              ⎰ Twins. Died in infancy.

        iii.   Eliza, ⎰

31. iv.   William Williams[5], b. in Dublin March 1, 1813. Married Alice West.

32. v.   Anne Williams[6], b. Oct. 24, 1818. Married Robert Whitla.

12. John Williams[5],

Son of Mathew Williams[4] and Ann Smith. Born about 1780 at the Groves. In John Williams'[4] will, he is referred to as "John Williams, of Coote Hill, County of Cavan." Died Jan. 10, 1808. Married ———, and left one daughter.

33.   i.   Matilda Williams[6], who married James Courtnay.

13. Mathew Williams[5],

Son of Mathew Williams[4], and Ann Smith. Born at the Groves, 1773. Married Mary Thompson, who was born Nov. 9, 1783, and died Oct. 9, 1868. He died July 20, 1837, aged 84 years. Had issue:

34.   i.   John Williams[6], b. 1807. Married Miss Guest:
35.   ii.   Matilda Williams, b. 1810. Married George Bartley.
36.   iii.   James Williams, b. Nov. 7, 1813. Married: 1. Martha Hamilton. 2. Dorothy Spence.
37.   iv.   Mary Williams, b. 1816. Married Josiah Dinely.
     v.   Mathew Williams, b. 1821. Died in England about 1856.

14. Sally Williams[5],

Daughter of Mathew Williams[4] and Ann Smith. Born at the Groves about 1775, and died at Cincinnati, O., about 1850. Married Woodney Browne. Had issue:

38.   i.   Ann Browne[9]. Married Hugh Simmons.

15. Margaret Williams[5],

Daughter of Mathew Williams[4] and Ann Smith. Born at the Groves about 1777. Married Mathew Browne.

     i.   Mathew Browne[6].
     ii.   A son, name unknown[6]. Lost at sea.
     Margaret (Williams) Browne died at Chillicothe, O.

16. Sarah Bell[6],

Daughter of Wm. Bell and Ann Williams[5]. Born at Emyvale, Monaghan County, Ireland, Aug. 20, 1769, and died at Louisville, Ky., Sept. 5, 1861. She married Aug. 31, 1792, James Anderson, and had issue:

     i.   William Bell Anderson[7], b. 1793. Married Eliza Reddick.
     ii.   Agnes Williams Anderson[7], b. 1796. Died unmarried, 1822.
     iii.   James Anderson, Jr.[7], b. Jan. 1, 1798. Married Caroline Brown.
     iv.   John Williams Anderson[7], b. Feb. 3, 1800. Married: 1. Elizabeth B. Runyan. 2. Anna M. McNair. 3. Elizabeth I. Gillis.
     v.   Janet Anderson[7], b. Jan. 13, 1804. Married Dr. Thomas Brown.
     vi.   Eleanor Anderson[7], b. 1806. Married Dr. Samuel Martin.
     vii.   Eliza Anderson[7], b. May, 1809. Died unmarried, 1835.

viii. George Wallace Anderson[7], b. Nov. 1812. Married Louisa Pettit.

ix. Mary Bell Anderson, b, March 12, 1818. Married Andrew Leach.

17. William Bell[6].

Son of William Bell and Ann Williams[5]. Born in Emyvale, Ireland, Feb. 11, 1781. Died Nov. 2, 1854, in the U. S. Married Margaret Van Horne Dwight. Had issue:

i. William Maurice Bell[7], b. October 17, 1812. Married Ann Brown.

ii. Walter Dwight Bell[7], b. Oct. 22, 1814. Married Elizabeth A. Richards.

iii. Sarah Ann Bell[7], b. Feb. 23, 1816. Married George Collier.

iv. Margaret De Witt Bell[7], b. Aug. 24, 1820. Married John L. Blaine.

v. Henry Rodgers Bell[7], b. May 29, 1822. Married Martha Jane Irwin.

vi. David Williams Bell[7], b. July 22, 1823.

vii. Algernon Sidney Bell[7], b. Aug. 8, 1825. Married Mary J. Park.

viii. Louisa Maria Bell[7], b. Aug. 20 1827. Married John R. Shepley.

ix. Catharine Ellen Bell[7], b. July 2, 1829. Married Rev. John V. Reynolds.

x. Elizabeth Woolsey Bell[7], b. Sept. 7, 1834.

(For a further account of this family, see "Dwight Genealogy, Vol. 1, p. 236.)

18. Samuel Bell[6].

Son of William Bell and Ann Williams[6]. Born in 1784 at Emyvale, Ireland, and died March, 1842, in Pennsylvania. Married Martha Ghormley. Had issue:

i. Mary Ann Bell[7]. Married Rev. Thomas McKinley.

ii. Nancy Bell[7]. Died single.

iii. Wm. Ghormley Bell[7]. Married Sarah Bell.

iv. Martha Bell[7].

v. Wiley Bell[7].

vi. Theodore Bell[7].

vii. [Seven? other children's names not recorded.]

Mr. Bell was married a second time to Miss Ann Jane Bell.

19. Ann Bell[6],

Ann Bell, daughter of William Bell and Ann Williams[5], was born at Emyvale, Ireland, 1786.   Died in 1810.   Married Cunningham S. Semple.   Had issue:

i.   Henry A. Semple[7].
ii.   Emeline Semple[7].   Married Rev. Samuel Tate.

20. Elizabeth Bell[6],

Elizabeth Bell, daughter of Wm. Bell and Ann Williams[5], was born in Emyvale, Ireland, 1789.   Died 1842.   She married 1, John Buchanan.   Had issue;

i.   Mary Ann Buchanan[7].   Married —— Patton.   Died childless.
2.   Married Dr. Rhodes Stansbury.   Had issue:
ii.   Elizabeth Stansbury.   Died single.
3.   Married —— Marshall.   Had issue:
iv.   William Marshall[7], of whom we have no account.

21. Samuel Williams[6],

Son of William Williams[5] and Margaret Widney.   Born in Carlisle, Pa., Oct. 16, 1786, and died in Cincinnati, O., Feb. 3, 1859. He married: 1. Eliza Armstrong (No. 27 of this record) and had issue:

i.   Mary Armstrong Williams[7], b. Sept. 8, 1810.   Married Samuel J. H. Abbot.
ii.   Edward Tiffin Williams[7], b. Jan. 2, 1815.   Married Elizabeth B. Williams.
iii.   Margaret Widney Williams[7], b. Apr. 9, 1817.   Married Wm. I. Ellsworth.
iv.   Eliza Jane Williams[7], b. Mar. 2, 1820.   Married Stephen Widney.
  Eliza (Armstrong) Williams died Mar. 3, 1820.   Samuel Williams married, 2. Margaret Troutner, and had issue:
v.   William George Williams[7], b. Feb. 25, 1822.   Married, 1. Mary Ann Davis.   2.   Delia Lathrop.
vi.   Helen Maria Williams[7], b. Aug. 3, 1824.   Died Nov. 2, 1824
vii.   Samuel Wesley Williams[7], b. Dec. 2, 1827.   Married Laura L. Evans.
viii.   John Fletcher Williams[7], b. Sept. 25, 1834.   Married Catherine Roberts.
  Mrs. Margaret (Troutner) Williams died Sept. 13, 1879,

in Springfield, O., aged 93 years. For further memoir of Samuel Williams see "Appleton's Cyclopedia of American Biography," vol. vi., or "Simpson's Cyclopedia of Methodism," p. 1004.

22. George Young Williams [6],

Son of William Williams[5] and Margaret Widney, was born at Path Valley, Pa., Oct. 11, 1788, and died at Chillicothe, O., Aug. 18, 1823. He married Mary Thompson. Had issue:

    i.   Louisa Williams[7], b. 1812. Married J. A. Brawner.

    ii. Thompson Williams[7], b. 1814. Married Elizabeth Lawson

    iii. William Williams[7], b. 1816. Died unmarried.

    iv. George Williams[7], Dec.14, 1818 } Twins. Died in infancy.

    v. Mary Williams[7],   " " " } Twins. Married George Reaugh.

    vi. John Williams, b. 1818. Married———— (?).

23. Mary Ann Williams [6],

Daughter of William Williams[5] and Margaret Widney, was born at Path Valley, Pa., Oct. 15th, 1792. Died in Dover, Tenn., June 14, 1843. She married William Bailey. Had issue:

    i.   Sarah Hall Bailey[7], b. Oct. 19, 1812. Married Wm. Kay.

    ii. John Williams Bailey[7], b. Dec. 13, 1854. Drowned May 25, 1819.

    iii. Margaret Widney Bailey[7], b. Oct. 15, 1817. Married James Rawley.

    iv. Mary Ann Eliza Bailey[7], b. Mar. 27. 1820. Married James Kay.

    v. William Williams Bailey[7], b. Nov. 23, 1822. Died Aug. 17, 1823.

    vi. Miranda Arabella Bailey[7], b. Dec. 27, 1825. Married A. G. Lee.

    vii. John Wesley Bailey[7], b. Sept. 17, 1830. Married Susan Wildbahn.

24. William Williams [6],

Son of William Williams[5] and Margaret Widney, was born in Franklin County, Pa., November 14, 1794. He married 1. Elizabeth Bayless. Had issue:

    i.   William Brown Williams[7], b. May 23, 1819. Died Sept. 7, 1819.

Married 2. Maria Caroline Buckingham, and had issue:

- ii. William Brown Williams 7, b. Aug. 16, 1822.   Married Helen M. Smith.
- iii. Elizabeth Bayless Williams 7, b. July 10, 1824.   Married Harvey M. Atkins.
- iv. Martha Williams 7, b. May 8, 1827.   Married Coleman Gatlin.
- vi. Margaret Widney Williams 7, b. Jan. 5, 1831.   Married John P. Dunlap.
- vii. George Young Williams 7, b. Feb. 20, 1834.   Killed at Chickamauga.
- viii. Mary Ann Williams 7, b. March 16, 1837.   Married S. P. Whitten.
- ix. Catharine Winston Williams 7, b. April 8, 1840.   Married Stacker Taylor.
- x. Amanda Caroline Williams 7, b. July 25, 1843.   Married H. H. Thorpe.
- xi. Sarah Frances Williams 7, b. Nov. 4, 1846.   Married Geo. L. Williams.

25. Jane Armstrong ,

Daughter of Thomas Armstrong and Mary Williams 5.   Born in Ireland.   Married James Campbell.   Had issue:

- i. Robert Campbell 7, b. in Ligonier, Pa.
- ii.–iii. Two daughters, names unknown.

26. John Armstrong 6,

Son of Thomas Armstrong and Mary Williams 5, b. in Ireland, 1779.   Married Rebecca Rule.   Had issue:

- i· William Armstrong 7, b. June 21, 1814.   Married Elizabeth Rule.
- ii. Sarah Jane Armstrong 7, b. 1818.   Died Nov. 9, 1855.
- iii. Charles Thomas Armstrong 7, b. May 9, 1824.   Married ———————— (?)
- iv. John Armstrong 7, b. June, 1835.   Died Nov. 19, 1835.

27. Eliza Armstrong 6,

See record of No. 21, Samuel Williams.

28. John Williams 6,

Son of Mathew Williams 5 and Margaret Bell.   Born in Lappan, Monaghan Co., Ireland, March 26, 1793, and died in Richmond,

Va., April 23, 1860. Married (in Richmond, Va.,) Sianna Armistead Dandridge. Had issue:

    i. Robert Alfred Williams[7]. Married Lizzie M. Colston.

    ii. Susan Eleanor Williams[7].

    iii. William Bell Williams[7]. Married Isabel M. Reed.

    iv. Margaret Sianna Williams[7]. Married P. H. Gibson.

    v. John Langbourne Williams[7]. Married Maria Ward Skelton.

28½. Thomas G. Williams[6],

Son of Mathew Williams[5] and Margaret Bell. Born in Va. Graduated at West Point. Appointed Lieut. in U. S. army, 1849. Resigned in 1861. Married —— ———————— and had issue:

    Several children, of whom we have no account.

29. Mathew Bell Williams[6],

Son of Mathew Williams[5] and Margaret Bell. Was born in Lappan, Monaghan Co., Ireland, Dec. 9, 1806. Married: 1. Margaret McAllister. Had issue:

    i. Ann E. Williams[7], b. June 20, 1833, in Philadelphia.

    ii. Mary Baine Williams[7], b. Aug. 7, 1835, in Shelby Co., O.

    iii. David Williams[7], b. April 8, 1837, in Shelby Co., O.

    iv. John Williams[7], b. Sept. 1, 1838, " " " "

    v. Edward McMay Williams, b. May 23, 1841, in Shelby Co., Ohio.

    vi. Margaret Bell Williams[7], b. Apr 1, 1843, in Shelby Co.,O.

2. Married Mrs. Brillina Wiley. Had issue:

    vii. Francis Johnson Williams[7], b. Feb. 11, 1853, in Shelby Co., Ohio.

    viii. Sarah Ann Williams[7].

    ix. Nancy Jane Williams[7].

30. John Alexander Williams[6],

Son of Alexander Williams[5] and Eliza Bocock. Born at Manchester, Eng., about 1805, and died at Cincinnati, O., 1855. Married Alice Pierson, and had issue:

    i. Hannah Williams[7].

    ii. Alexander Williams[7].

    iii. John Alexander Williams[7]. Drowned at Cincinnati 1855.

    iv. William Williams[7].

    v. George Pierson Williams[7].

    vi. Alice Williams[7]. Married Thomas James, d. in Brooklyn, N. Y., 1887.

    vii. Elizabeth Anne Williams[7].

31. William Williams[6],

Son of Alexander Williams[5] and Eliza Bocock. Born in Dublin March 1, 1813. Married July 12, 1845, Alice West. Mrs. W. died 1867. Had issue:

 i. Alexander Williams[7], b. in 1846.
 ii. Edward Williams[7], b. in 1848.
 iii. Eliza Williams[7].
 iv. Eleanor Williams[7].
 v. William John Williams, b. 1860.

 Mr. Williams' address is No. 2 Dame St. Dublin.

32. Anne Williams[6],

Daughter of Alexander Williams[5] and Eliza Bocock. Was born at Dublin, Oct. 24, 1818. Married Aug. 9, 1841, at Monaghan, Robbert Whitla. Their issue:

 i. Eliza Whitla[7], b. Nov. 29, 1842. Died May, 1843.
 ii. James Whitla[7], b. April 16, 1844. Married Charlotte Duncan. Died June 26, 1879.
 iii. Alexander Whitla[7], b. April 15, 1845. Married Pollie Williams.
 iv. Robert Jones Whitla[7], b. April 22, 1846. Married Miss Wright.
 v. Sarah Whitla[7], b. March 27, 1848. Died May 18, 1871.
 vi. Eliza Anne Whitla[7], b. Dec. 27, 1849. Married James Gracey.
 vii. William Whitla[7], b. Sept. 13, 1851. Married Edith Bourne.
 viii. Anne Whitla[7], b. Dec. 18, 1852. Died Nov. 18, 1880.
 ix. Alice Whitla[7], b. April 17, 1854. Married Rev. John Cushing.
 x. Maggie Whitla[7], b. Jan. 8, 1856.
 xi. Meredith Whitla[7], b. Nov. 27, 1858. Married May Connor.
 xii. Rachel Whitla[7], b. Sept. 12, 1860.

 The address of Mr. Whitla is Monaghan, Ireland.

33. Matilda Williams[6],

Daughter of John Williams [5] "of Coote Hill," and —— ——. Married James Courtnay. Had issue:

 i. Mary Ann Courtnay[7].
 ii. Matilda Courtnay[7].

iii. Jane Courtnay[7]. Married Robert Sharp. Died at Horwellsville, N. Y., Dec 12, 1877, aged 47 years.

iv. Ellen Courtnay[7].

v. Margaret Courtnay[7].

vi. Harriette Courtnay[7].

vii. Olivia Courtnay[7].

34. John Williams[6],

Son of Mathew Williams[5] and Mary Thompson. Born at the Groves, March 26, 1807. Married Miss Guest, and had issue:

i. Amelia Charlotte Williams[7].

ii. Mary Jane Williams[7].

iii. Charlotte Victoria Williams[7].

iv. John Williams[7].   Died in infancy.

v. Isabella Susannah Williams[7].   Died in infancy.

vi. Matilda Amelia Williams[7].   "   "   "

vii. Eliza Ann Williams[7].   "   "   "

viii. Georgianna Wiiliams[7].   "   "   "

John Williams died Dec. 6, 1871.

35. Matilda Williams[6],

Daughter of Mathew Williams[5] and Mary Thompson. Born at Dublin, 1810. Died about 1860. Married at Gingory, George Bartley, Jan. 11, 1839. Had issue:

i. William Bartley .

ii. George Bartley

iii. Eliza Bartley .

36. James Williams[6],

Son of Mathew Williams[5] and Mary Thompson. Born Nov. 7, 1813, at Milltown, Dublin. Married: 1. Martha Hamilton. Had issue:

i. Andrew Hamilton Williams[7], b. June 30, 1852. Lives in N. Y.

ii. James Thompson Williams[7], b. Feb. 5, 1854. Died April 26, 1877.

iii. Robert Stanley Williams[7], b. Nov.19, 1855. Lives in N. Y.
2. Married Dorothy Spence. Had issue:

iv. Martha Emma Williams[7], b. Oct. 1, 1862.

v. Dora Williams[7], b. Feb. 3, 1864.

Mr. James Williams address is 43 Dame st., Dublin.

37. Mary Williams[6],

Daughter of Mathew Williams[5] and Mary Thompson. Born at Donnybrook, Dublin, May, 1818. Married Josiah Dinely, of Gingory, Nov. 5, 1840. Had issue:

    i.   Josiah Dinely[7], b. Sept. 16, 1841.

    ii. Rachel Dinely[7], b. March 4, 1844, at Lancaster, Eng.

    iii. Andrew Thompson Dinely[7], b. Nov. 25, 1845, at Castleshane.

38. Ann Browne[6],

Daughter of Sally Williams[5] and Woodney Browne, Married Hugh Simmons, and removed to Cincinnati, O. They had issue:

    i.   Sarah Simmons[7]. Died 1831, aged 17 years.

    ii.   Child[7], name unknown Died —— (?) aged 9 years.

    iii. Charlotte Simmons[7]. Died 1831, aged 10 years.

    iv. Maria Simmons[7]. Married —— Drew.

    v.   Hannah Matilda Simmons[7]. Married —— Duncan.

    vi. Ann Elizabeth Simmons[7]. Died in 1831, aged 4 years.

    vii. Robert Bailey Simmons[7].

   viii. John Simmons[7].

    ix. Hugh Simmons[7].